Summary:

The 5 Second Rule

TRANSFORM YOUR LIFE, WORK, AND CONFIDENCE WITH EVERYDAY COURAGE

EpicRead

© *2019*

Contents

Courage; /'kerij/

Noun

- **The ability to do something that is difficult or scary**
- **Stepping outside of your comfort zone**
- **Sharing your ideas, speaking up, or showing up**
- **Standing firm in your beliefs and values**
- **And some days...getting out of bed.**

The 5 Second Rule

The moment you have an instinct to act on a goal you must 5-4-3-2-1 and physically move or your brain will stop you!

Part 1-The 5 Second Rule

Five Seconds to Change Your Life

Your life can be changed with one 5-second decision at a time and this is a science that will be proven in this book. The 5-second rule will help you live, love, work and will boost your confidence and courage. It can be easily learned and has a profound impact. Once you start using it, it will be there for you whenever you need it. The author discovered this rule when she was at a very low point in her life and was so distressed that the simple act of getting out of the bed was a struggle. Her initial thoughts about the rule were that it was silly but little did she realize that she has invented a powerful metacognition tool that could change absolutely everything about a person's life.

Since discovering this rule, the author has taken control of her life and improved her cash flow, marriage and career. She has cured herself of anxiety, built and sold two businesses and has become one of the most-booked speakers in the world. She has never been more happy, in control or free. She has replaced her tendency to overthink with a bias towards action and has used the rule to master self-monitoring and become more present in the moment. It also taught her to start believing in herself and gave her the strength to become a better and happier person.

The 5-second rule brings about this change by teaching you one simple thing; HOW to change. This rule will help wake up your inner genius, leader, rock star, athlete, artist and change agent as well as help you wake up at time. This book is full of real-life experiences of people who used this rule in unique ways to take charge of their lives. This implies that the rule is limitless in its usefulness and application.

You can use this rule to become more productive and influential at work, step out of your comfort zone, become more effective at networking, self-monitor as well as control your emotions and help with addictions and depressions. It might even save the life of someone. Executives within the world's most respectable brands are taking the help of this rule to make their managers incorporate change, drive sales, engage teams and innovate. We face countless scary and uncertain moments in our daily lives which is why dealing with it requires courage. This rule will help you find the courage to become your greatest self. We all possess greatness inside of us and the rule will help us hear that greatness with clarity even in the weakest of moments as well as the courage to act on it.

The author has built Real Confidence by learning to honor their instincts with action so that they come to life. It is only through action that she has been able to unlock the power inside her to become the person she always wanted to be. This transformation can be experienced by anyone if they practice the 5-

second rule consistently. Each time you use it, you will become closer to being the person you are truly meant to be. Moreover, once you start using it, you will be astonished at how easy it is to make a 5-second decision that changes everything.

The author always wondered why changing things was so hard even when it was for the better. However, after she started practicing the 5-second rule, she realized that change came down to the courage one needs every day to make small 5-second decisions. As she used the rule more and more, she realized that she was making small decisions all day long that held her back. In the end, 5-seconds of courage make all the difference. When you act with courage, your brain is not involved. Your heart speaks first and you listen. And when you truly reflect on this, you realize that you must have made several 'heart-first' decisions in your life where you ignored your fear and let your courage and your confidence speak for you.

How she discovered the 5-second rule

Starting in 2009, the author was 41 years of age and dealing with major problems in relation to money, work and marriage when she discovered the 5-second rule. She dreaded waking up and getting out of bed. Moreover, overthinking was making her problems worse and she was stuck in a 'habit-loop' where she had hit the snooze button so many times that the habit was encoded in her brain. Mornings at her home were a total chaos when the school bus would leave without picking the children up and she would wake up long after her husband had left for work. It was a common routine for her to forget the kids' lunches, backpacks and permission slips as she hurried to drop them off to school. Her self-confidence was in a death spiral and she was losing hope for any betterment in her life. Surprisingly, the HARDEST things in her case were to get up on time, being nice to her husband and asking for help from family and friends, all VERY simple acts. And even though she knew she needed to change things, she just didn't know how.

However, everything changed one day when she saw a TV commercial with a rocket launching on the count of 5, 4, 3, 2, 1...It was the instant that she decided she would 'launch' herself out of the bed the next morning, moving so fast that there would be no time to talk herself out of it. This instinct to launch herself was her inner wisdom talking whereas hearing it was a tipping point and following it was life-changing.

Research shows that there is a strong connection between your brain and your instinct to act which is why the brain fires up your instincts whenever there is an opportunity to achieve your goals. This is why it is extremely important to pay attention to your instincts and to honor them with action because they are voiced by your wisdom which is a genius when it comes to your goals, dreams and major life-changes. Subconsciously, the author's brain was signaling her to pay attention to the rocket launch on TV and was sending her clear instructions to grab the idea, believe in it and execute it.

The author feels extremely thankful that she followed this idea because the next morning she launched herself out of the bed, just as planned and despite feeling dread and stupid at the thought of counting backwards and pushing the covers aside. However, she ignored her feelings, did not think and acted on what needed to be done. That was the exact moment that she discovered the 5-second rule.

What you can expect when you use it
At first, the author was pleasantly surprised that something so stupid worked. However, she just knew that it helped her wake up on time

despite trying to do so in vain for months and made changing her behavior simple. It was only later that she found out that when you count backwards, you mentally shift the gears in your mind, interrupting your default thinking and 'asserting control'. It distracts the mind from excuses and changes your physiology, making your mind fall back in line. It is a 'starting ritual' that activates the prefrontal cortex, helping to change your behavior. The prefrontal cortex is the part of brain responsible for focus, change and deliberate action.

The author kept using the rule the next morning successfully and then started to experience 5-second moments all day long. If she stopped to think what she was about to do, she would lose focus but as long as she used the 5-second rule she was good. The rule worked because all it took was five seconds for her brain to drown her thoughts in a flood of excuses and stop her from acting on her instincts. Therefore, she made a promise to herself that she would use the rule whenever her instincts would tell her that she should do something that would change her for the better.

There is a 5 second window between the initial instinct to act and your brain stopping you which is why it is crucial that you act within these 5 seconds. Pushing yourself to take simple actions creates a chain reaction in your confidence and productivity whereas the more you believe you are in control of your life, the happier and more successful you will be and a bias towards action is sure to achieve just that. The rule does not make these things easy, it makes them happen which is why the author describes it as a tool. It helps provide users a framework, the courage and methods for HOW to push themselves to change.

In the process of deconstructing the moment of change, the author realized that hesitation is the kiss of death which triggers a mental system designed to stop you. If you stop hesitating and take 'some kind of action', you will be amazed at how fast your life changes. Every phase of your life and career demands a different you and using the rule will help you become that person.

Why the rule works
The rule is a simple yet research-backed metacognition tool that creates immediate and lasting behavior change. All you have to do is to count backwards from 5 and MOVE as soon as you reach 1. You should practice this whenever

there is something **you know you should do** but feel uncertain or fearful about.

Counting backwards will distract you from worries, focus your attention on what needs to be done, prompting you to act while interrupting the habit of hesitation and overthinking. Both counting and moving are actions. When you teach yourself to take action instead of stopping to think, you can create remarkable change. Moreover, it does not work if you count forwards because then you keep counting. On the contrary, when you count backwards, there is nowhere to go after counting 1 so it becomes a prompt to move.

The author started with a count of five because it seemed just the right amount of time to give herself to act. There are other 5-second rules in the world as well and all of them are based on a common premise; they require a person to physically move within a 5-second window. This 5 second window seems to work for everyone, however, you can play around with it to make it work for you. You can shorten or lengthen it to personalize so that it creates the maximum utility for you. Nonetheless, you must realize that the longer you think about something, the lower your urge to act becomes.

You GOT to move fast, before your mind paralyzes you.

The rule may also seem very similar to Nike's tagline "Just Do It!", however, while "Just Do It!" refers to WHAT you need to do, the 5-second rule tells you HOW to do it which is why it is considered a tool as opposed to a concept. The reason Nike's tagline is the most famous in the world is because it uses the word "Just". It acknowledges that while we are all struggling with pushing ourselves to be better and do better, we all hesitate and struggle with feelings that direct us to do the opposite. It tells us that we are not alone in this struggle but that we should be bigger than it. It is pushing us to move past doubt and get in the game. It also resonates profoundly with us because ALL of us, even the most successful and accomplished athletes, need a PUSH. And the rule tells us exactly how to give ourselves that push. By counting 5-4-3-2-1 and moving!

What can I use it for?

1. It can be used to change your behaviors and to push yourself to create new habits while pulling away from destructive ones. It can also be used to master the skills of

self-monitoring and self-control. This will in turn make you more effective and intentional in your relationships.

2. The rule can be used to discover courage to do new, scary or uncertain things. It will quiet your self-doubt and build confidence.

3. The rule can be used to control negative thoughts and worries that cloud your mind as well as break the habit of anxiety and beat fears. Once you regain control of your mind, you will be able to think about things that bring joy instead of sorrow and depression.

Why does something so simple work?

The rule works because of its simplicity. Great researchers have concluded that the moment you want to change or break a habit or do something hard or scary, your brain goes on to stop you and trick you into thinking things through. These tricks also include things like cognitive biases, paradox of choice, psychological immune system and the spotlight effect. This gets you trapped into your own thoughts because your mind is scared of things that are uncertain, scary or new. Therefore, this reluctance is hard-wired into you and happens really fast which is why it is crucial that you act faster.

The rule also exemplifies some proven principles in modern phycology including internal locus of control, starting rituals, a bias towards action and the Golden Rule of Habits, amongst a few. The 5 second rule actually only works on one thing; YOU. It's you who stop yourself from changing by first hesitating, then overthinking and finally locking yourself up in mental jail. Hesitation sends stress signals to your brain which makes it turn on protection mode. This is exactly how we are wired to fail.

However, hesitation can also be used to your advantage since it opens the 5-second window which can be used to push yourself forward. Furthermore, seeing the countdown anywhere in display can be extremely helpful in reminding you of the rule and its importance.

Can the rule create lasting behavior change too? We are unaware that patterns of thinking like worrying, self-doubt and fear are all habits which can be broken down with the help of latest research. Once you start practicing the 5-second rule, its countdown 5-4-3-2-1-GO will become your new behavior pattern. It will beat your brain's operating system and with continuous practice destroy it altogether. It will also become a 'starting ritual' that will interrupt your bad default patterns and trigger new positive ones, reprogramming your mind. The 'Golden Rule of Habits' illustrates that in order to change a pattern of any bad habit, you must replace it and this is exactly what the rule will help you do. As you put it into practice, the 5-second rule will prevent you from defaulting into worry and hesitation and you will automatically start acting with courage.

With the passage of time as you will practice this rule even more, you will discover real confidence and pride in yourself. You can change your default mental settings one 5-second decision at a time which will ultimately lead to major changes in who you are, what you feel and how you live. If you think that your habits, mindset and personality are set in stone then fortunately you are wrong because these are flexible and this fact has some very powerful implications for your life.

Change your decisions and you'll change your life. And what will change your decisions more than anything? Courage.

Every day Courage

Courage in not limited to the acts of historical personalities such as Galileo and Muhammad Ali. Rather it is characterized by facing scary and uncertain moments in everyday life and unlocking opportunity and joy. Being courageous is sometimes as simple as getting out of bed on time, speaking to your boss or stepping on a scale.

As the author started doing research on the historical moments of courage in an attempt to understand its nature even better, she came across the story of Rosa Parks who refused to give up her bus seat for a white passenger. This small act of hers sparked the American Civil Rights Movement and teaches us that it is not the big moves in life that change everything. Rosa's decision to stand up to mistreatment wasn't one that she thought through, neither was that of Dr. Martin Luther King Jr., who accepted the nomination to lead the boycott of Mrs. Rosa's arrest and later became one of the greatest civil rights leader of all times. Mrs. Rosa was a person who tried her best to stay out of trouble and only meant to get back to her home the evening of the incident. Similarly, Dr. Martin Luther King Jr. was a young preacher at the time he was nominated to lead the Montgomery Improvement Association and a 381-day protest against the arrest of Mrs. Rosa. Both of them experienced the power of the push when your instincts, values and goals align and you move so quickly that you do not have the chance to talk yourself out of it.

In an interview in 1956, Rosa Parks explained that she was pushed as far as she could stand to be pushed. However, in the moment that she took stand for herself, she was pushed by something greater-herself. This is what courage is. It is a push.

Greatness is not a personality trait and is found inside all of us. Just like a shy and quiet person like Mrs. Parks had not thought that she would be the person to do it, you are also unaware of what great things you are capable of achieving at work and in your life. Courage is a **birthright which is inside all of us**. It is not dependent on anything except you knowing how to find it when you need it. Remember, you don't have to have all the answers. You just need to make a decision in the next five seconds. And you may be alone when you need it the most. You will know that it is a push moment when you suddenly get the instinct to act and your feelings scream NO at the same time. There are various real-life examples that highlight the struggle between our desire to change our lives and our fear of it. They also reveal the power that everyday courage has to transform everything.

When we think about being courageous, we focus on the solution rather the problem. That tiny switch that pushes us from being fearful to being courageous is mentally liberating. When you push yourself, you may not bring a drastic change in the world around you but you will change yourself which is something equally important.

There is only one YOU.

And there will never be another one.

That's your power.

What are you waiting for?
All the reasons and excuses that you are using to hold yourself back are wrong. There is no 'right time' to improve your life neither is it futile to try or better to keep peace. The moment you move you will discover your strength and bring your real self to the world

and the best time to do it is right now when your heart tells you to move.

We all hold ourselves back and hide away because we are afraid even to try. We dodge challenges to protect our egos even if it means eliminating the possibility of getting what we want and waste an enormous amount of time for the right moment to take action. As the famous quote says, "You miss 100% of the shots you don't take".

Life is already tough and we make it tougher by listening to our fears and doubts. We hold ourselves back because we are afraid to even try.

We need to ask ourselves one crucial question;

WHAT IF WE ARE WRONG?

Although it is such a powerful question, we rarely ask it ourselves. What if we are wrong in assuming that we are not as good as others? What if you not only meet your goals for the year but also surpass them? And what if being single is not as scary as it seems and your soulmate is just waiting for you around the corner?

Even if you do suck, you can say yourself;

SO WHAT!?

At least you tried!

Whether or not you were able to achieve what you wanted does not matter as much as trying to achieve it in the first place. The only thing relevant is you and you hold all the power that is required to help you succeed in this world. However, the only way to access that power is to push yourself to try.

You can never stop yourself from worrying over things. However, you can stop yourself from letting those worries drag you into a parade that controls your mind. You can instead push yourself to think about something empowering and step back into the present moment and go for what you want.

In five seconds flat.

We are all waiting for the 'right time' in utter stupidity. Moreover, we are all guilty of thinking about getting involved but not doing it. Our greatest heroes also needed to be pushed through their fears, excuses and feelings just like us because all human beings are wired this way. It is our feelings and fears that convince us that now is not the right time and keep us from achieving greatness.

So are you waiting for someone to push and drag you to do what needs to be done? Sometimes there is no next chance and no time out. It is now or never. Sometimes you are not procrastinating while waiting and by convincing yourself that now is not the time, you are deliberately working against your dreams.

You may think you are protecting yourself from judgement or rejection but in reality you are limiting your ability to make your dreams come true when you make excuses and talk yourself into waiting. You may convince yourself that you are afraid of finding out that you suck, however, what sucks even more is being older and regretting that you never went for it. There is no 'right time', there is only 'right now'. You get only one life and it is not going to begin again. It's up to you to push yourself to make the most of it and the time to do it is right now. Don't wait!

You validate your ideas by pursuing them

Waiting for validation will be the death of your dreams. The world rewards those who are courageous enough to stop waiting and start. The person who has the courage to start, create and put themselves and their ideas out there is the one who will win. And the best way to start is to get out of your comfort zone and begin.

When you sit with fear and uncertainty, your mind makes it expand. This is called the 'Spotlight effect' and it's one of the tricks of your brain to keep you 'Safe'. You can feel uncertain and be ready and you can be afraid and do it anyway.

Five seconds of courage changes everything

The treasure in your life is buried inside you. It's not inside someone else. You are the source of power in your life which can be unlocked when you listen to your instincts and push yourself to honor them. When you discover your 'inner true self', it will be the most important gift of all. There is no debate when you follow your heart and a decision to move will automatically quieten the chatter in your mind. If you want to make your dreams come true, get ready for the long game. Success is a numbers game and you are not going to win if you keep telling yourself to wait. The more often you choose courage, the more likely you'll succeed. Once you open yourself up to the opportunity this world has to offer, you will discover the power inside you even if you are unable to achieve what you wanted.

You'll never feel like it

Without ever realizing it, we make almost every single decision in our life with our feelings. And our feelings in the moment are almost never aligned with what is best for us. Once you understand the role feelings play in your decision making, you will be able to beat them. Feelings decide for us 95% of the time. Neuroscientist Antonio Damasio says that human beings are 'feeling machines that think' not 'thinking machines that feel'. His study of people with damage to their brains and who were unable to feel any emotions revealed that they were unable to make a decision even though they knew what was logical to do. Our feelings are so overpowering that if we only act when we feel like it, we will never get what we want. It is vital that you learn to separate what you feel from the actions that you take and the 5-second rule will help you achieve just that. You cannot control how you feel but you can always choose how you act.

Feelings are merely suggestions that the greatest athletes ignore. You must do the same if you want to change. We and the most successful people in this world all battle with the same self-defeating feelings. The only difference is how we tackle these and get ourselves to take action.

Confidence is a skill that you build through action. The 5-second rule is your ally and a tool for action for behavior change aligned with your goals and commitments. You must push right through the feelings that stop you and do the work to break the habits that hold you back. Afterwards, you must replace those habits with habits of courage.

At the heart of everyday courage is a choice. There is a very strong bond between courage and confidence because every courageous move grows your confidence, one 5-second decision at a time.

How to start using the rule
Change is simple, not easy. A very simple challenge to work your way towards the 5-second rule is to set your morning alarm for 30 minutes earlier and then 5-4-3-2-1 push yourself out of the bed. This challenge is important because there is no wiggle room in it since it only involves you, your alarm and the 5-second rule. Secondly, if you can change your morning routine, you can change anything. This is because if you can master the art of acting deliberately despite of how you feel in one area

of life, you can do the same in any other area. This challenge in also crucial since the initial amount of energy required to push yourself out of bed is much higher than that needed once you are up and running.

If you don't get that push in the morning, your brain will ultimately convince you to do nothing. When you get up as soon as the alarm rings, you unleash personal power. This proves that you have the inner strength to do what needs to be done. If you cannot get yourself out of the bed then you will not be able to pursue all of the other changes that you want to make in your life. Taking control of your mornings will catalyze a chain reaction that will lead to change everywhere.

If you can get up on time, start your day powerfully, plan ahead, think about your goals, and focus on yourself, all before getting bogged down by your daily routine, then you will simply accomplish more. This is the first step to taking control of your life.

The 5-second rule is 'change agnostic' and will work with any kind of behavior change that you want. We constantly receive questions about health, productivity and procrastination from people which is why these are specifically discussed in detail. You will not only learn the secret to improving your health with the help of 5-second rule but will also learn about how to increase your productivity as well as a step-by-step method to beat the two forms of procrastination.

All of these strategies are backed by science, however, in order to benefit from them you will have to push yourself because there is no other way.

Either you run the day or the day runs you.

Improve your health

You can use the 5-second rule to address any of the health concerns you have. Merely thinking about being healthy won't help you which is why you must take action to work towards a healthy body and mind. Any diet would work if you follow it but the problem is not the diet itself but your feelings about dieting.

The moment you accept the fact that we just want to do the things that feel easy, you will realize that the secret to getting healthier is to 5-4-3-2-1-GO! because you will never feel like it. Getting healthy is only made so much harder by your feelings. Exercise is 100% mental because your body won't go where your mind does not push it. That is why the 5-second rule is game changing for your health because it will help you get past your cravings and laziness and push you to do what is necessary to achieve a healthy body and mind.

It takes courage to start something, it takes courage to stick with it, and it definitely takes courage to share it with the world. Feeling that it is impossible to bridge the gap between where you are now and what you want to become is normal. However, allowing those feelings to take over your mind is a form of self-abuse.

It takes courage to be honest with yourself about what you want. It also takes courage to assert yourself and start. The first step is hard and slipping is normal. But you must remember that you can regain control in 5 seconds. The author wanted you to undertake the wakeup challenge so you can experience 'activation energy' which is the energy required to start something. The 5-second rule is also a tool that can be used to find the inner strength to face serious illness.

Improving your health is all about action. You can push yourself to do small things such as visiting your doctor or the dentist and getting a mammogram done. Life is about the choices we make and you can always choose how you act. What you need to do is simple but it will never be easy. However, it will be worth it. Remember, you don't have to feel like it, you just have to do it.

Go the extra mile. It's never crowded.

Increase Productivity

Productivity can be boiled down to one word-FOCUS. Focus has two types; first, you need the ability to manage distractions so you can focus on the task on hand and second, you need to master the skill of focusing on the bigger picture so that you don't waste time on stupid stuff.

Managing distractions also requires you to ignore what you feel and instead do what is necessary. Even though you are well aware of how these distractions divert you away from achieving your goals, you would not want to manage them which is why you have to PUSH yourself to do this.

First, you must decide that distractions are not good. Any sort of interruptions are the kiss of death for your productivity. You just have to decide that your goals are more important than push notifications. Next, you must remove these distractions.

5-4-3-2-1- Remove the distractions. It is that simple.

Own your mornings

Taking control of your mornings is a game changer for productivity. By creating a morning routine and following it, you 'set your intentions'. According to Duke University professor Dan Ariely, the first two to three hours of the day are the best for your brain once you fully wake up. For peak productivity, you should NEVER hit the snooze button. Scientists recently discovered that hitting the snooze button has a negative impact on the brain function and productivity that can last for up to four hours.

The science behind this is something like this. We sleep in cycles of 90 to 110 minutes.

However, these cycles end and our bodies become ready to wake up two hours before the wake up time. If we hit the snooze button once our alarm rings, we are actually pushing our bodies to induce a new sleep cycle that will last for another 90-110 minutes. It can take up to four hours for this 'sleep inertia' to wear off and for your cognitive functions to return to their full capacity. This is the reason you wake up extremely groggy after you have hit the snooze button.

The author makes it a habit of putting an alarm and then placing her phone in the bathroom so that she does not have access to it to push snooze or check notifications. Moreover, she does not check the phone until after she has planned her day so that she can prioritize her own goals before anyone else's. She has also developed a habit of writing her goals for the day since you are 42% more likely to achieve your objectives if you jot them down.

She also uses a strategy called 30 before 7:30 whereby she takes 30 minutes before 7:30 am to plan her day or to start on the most important tasks on her to-do list. By planning your day such that you focus on the right things prime yourself to be much more productive and successful. It is critical that you plan your day BEFORE you walk into your office or answer the first email/call of the day because once you do that, you are interrupted and as stated earlier, interruption is the kiss of death for productivity.

Furthermore, she also plans her quitting time when she would stop all work and spend the rest of her time with family. This is important because it gets her intentional with the time she has and makes her more productive. A principle called 'Parkinson's law' states that work expands to whatever time you give it which is why it is extremely important to give your workday a deadline in order to preserve stamina and mental health.

What the author is telling you is simple, obvious and shows results. You can customize it so it works for you and may add meditation and gratitude lists to your morning routine.

Start before you're ready. Don't prepare, begin.

End procrastination

Procrastination has two types; destructive and productive procrastination. Productive procrastination, as the name implies, is a good form of procrastination which is necessary during a creative process in order to let your mind wander. This provides the ability to come up with more productive ideas. If you are not getting the results you want, give the project some time, go focus your energy somewhere else and return with fresh perspective. The fresh ideas that you get as a result of productive procrastination will make your work even smarter.

Destructive procrastination, in the other hand, is an entirely different animal. It occurs when we ignore the work that needs to be done and know that there will be negative consequences of this ignorance. It's anything that we find ourselves deliberately avoiding that really needs to get done. Also, while we all incorrectly thought procrastination to be a form of laziness, it is in fact a coping mechanism for stress.

Procrastination and the connection to stress
According to a psychology professor who studied procrastination for 19 years, procrastination is not about avoiding work rather it is about avoiding stress. It is a subconscious desire to feel good right now so you can avoid stress later. Most of the people who procrastinate have no control over it

because they do not know the real reason behind why they procrastinate. It is a way for people to take a mini stress-break from the bigger stress you feel overall.

The more often you procrastinate, the more of a habit it will become. While it is initially an attempt to avoid stress, it later builds more stress because the work you have been avoiding piles up. When we replace a difficult task with something that is easier to do, we get a temporary mood boost and a feeling of control.

In order to combat procrastination, you must first begin with forgiving yourself. A part of the problem of procrastination is that such people are extremely hard on themselves. Research also proves that when you can picture the 'future you', it gives you the objectivity to push yourself in the present moment. This then becomes the next step in battling procrastination. You must envision the future you and then think about what that future version would have done when you are faced with procrastination. Then finally, once you understand the source of procrastination, create a 'starting ritual'. There is no better starting ritual than the 5-second rule. The 5-second rule works because it helps you create new habits (getting started) when you are stuck in procrastination. Moreover, while procrastination makes you feel like you have no control over yourself, the 5-second rule helps you take back that control and makes you feel empowered. Each time you use the rule, it will become easier and easier to stop procrastinating.

Getting started is also extremely important because it gets you involved in the 'progress principle' which describes the phenomenon that a forward progress of any kind boosts our mood and increases our happiness and productivity. It also gets our brain to cue us to keep at it since we have initiated the process of achieving something. Researchers have found out that the brain remembers unfinished tasks more than the finished ones. This book repeatedly advocates that unless you beat the feelings that trigger your bad habits and you push yourself to get started, you'll never change.

You'll either find a way or you'll find an excuse.

How to become the happiest person you know

The upcoming content will help you understand how to use the 5-second rule in combination with some recent research-based strategies to beat fear, stop worrying and manage or cure anxiety. The author explains that she developed her confidence by practicing acts of everyday courage over the years. She explains her struggle of dealing with anxiety and how she thought about using the 5-second rule to change her thoughts. She had witnessed the effect of the rule on other habits which made her think why not to use it to break the mental habit of anxiety, panic and fear?

Resultantly, she started using it to break the habit of worrying, control her anxiety and beat the fear of flying. The rule helped her to the extent that she stopped taking medication for anxiety and became panic-attack free. Learning to take control of her mind, direct her thoughts and dismantle fear greatly improved the quality of her life. She has transformed herself by practicing this rule and has been the happiest and most optimistic that she has ever been.

The solution to anxiety, fear and excessive worrying is as follows. For dealing with mind-numbing worry, you must break the habit of worrying and negative self-talk using the 5-second rule, the science of habits and the power of gratitude. For managing anxiety, you must learn about what anxiety actually comprises of as well as follow a step-by-step method to reframe, interrupt and eventually eliminate it for good. Lastly for beating any kind of fear, you must learn to use the 5-second rule with 'anchor thoughts' to prevent fear from taking over your mind.

Life is amazing.

And then it's awful.

And then it's amazing again.

And in between the amazing and the awful,

it's ordinary and mundane and routine.

Breathe in the amazing, hold on through

the awful, and relax and exhale

during the ordinary. That's just living.

Heartbreaking, soul-healing, amazing,

awful, ordinary life. And it's

breathtakingly beautiful.

-LR Knost

Stop worrying

Ending the habit of worrying will have the single biggest positive impact on your life because it is something that we have learnt from our childhood. Consequently as adults, we spend too much time and energy worrying about things that are out of our control or that could go wrong. Worrying has become the default setting which your mind goes to when you are not paying attention. Research shows that the biggest regret of people nearing the end of their lives was that they wish they had not spent so much of their lifetime worrying. Their advice to others was that worry is an enormous waste of your limited and precious lifetime. The solution is to catch yourself as you are drifting into worry and then regaining mental control by using the rule.

When you first begin to use the 5-second rule to end your habit of worrying, you will be amazed at how often your mind just drifts to something negative. You will most probably have to fight it every day.

Feelings of love often trigger worry

Although the feelings of worry are subtle, they can seize control of you really fast. The author notices that she particularly starts to worry the moment that she feels happiness or love. She quotes her experience with her daughter where she would find her heart swell with love when she saw her sleeping as an infant or witnessed her in a beautiful gown for her prom. In moments like these, she would think that her heart would burst with the love she felt for her daughter. However, right afterwards, she would be filled with worry and dreadful thoughts which would steal the moment and grip her with fear. Worry robbed her of joy in moments like these and instead of just being present and admiring the love for her daughter, she would be taken to a dark place in her mind.

This is the same way worries and fear hijack your mind and rob you of the magic and wonder in your life. Feeling the worst-case scenario in moments of joy is very common and it is so hard for us to soften into joy because we are trying to beat vulnerability to the punch. When your mind takes you somewhere dark, sad and negative, you don't have to go with it.

The 5-second rule is what will help you regain control in moments like these. The counting will yank you out of your head and plant you in the present moment. It will switch your gears from worry to focus. It is also helpful to ask yourself

'What am I grateful for?' in moments like these. As soon as you think about what you are grateful for, you will start feeling grateful instead of worried and focus on the positive aspects of your life. Nothing is perfect in life but you can use the 5-second rule to silence the chatter going on in your mind. Feeling grateful also changes your brain chemistry, according to neuroscientist Alex Korb. It activates the brainstem region that produces dopamine.

It's okay to be scared. Being scared means you're about to do something really, really brave.

End anxiety

When your habit of worrying gets out of control, it leads to anxiety. However, as crippling as it may seem, you can use the 5-second rule in combination with a strategy called 'reframing' to combat this issue. The key to beating anxiety is catching it in its initial phases. Once you let it spiral out of control, it will turn into full-blown panic. As you practice the 5-second rule even more to put your anxiety to rest, it will weaken and reduce to its original form-worries. Afterwards, you can use the 5-second rule and gratitude to eliminate worry.

Normal panic vs panic attacks

We face tons of moments in our life when we feel panicked. It happens every time you encounter a "near miss" whereby you get saved by luck. In moments like these, your heart races, breathing speeds up and cortisol surges. These are just coping mechanisms for your body to prepare you for taking control of the situation. Once your body is in panic mode, your brain is triggered to find a reason and once it finds a reasonable justification for your body to be acting up, it understands the situation and won't escalate anxiety. Once the danger has passed, your mind will signal your body to calm down and you will just be cautious for the next time.

On the contrary, when you have a panic attack, you will have adrenaline surge through your body without any reason. You might just be busy in doing your everyday chores when it will attack you and your body will go into a state of hyper alertness. Now when the mind is triggered to find a reason for your hyper alertness and it won't find any, it will think you must be in actual danger and escalate the fear, thinking that the danger is imminent. The lack of a reason will make the anxiety worse and you will want to physically run away from the situation.

Trying to calm down does not work

Trying to 'change the channel' and thinking about something else will not help full-blown anxiety. This is because when you feel anxious, you are in a state of physical agitation. Asking you to calm down in this situation is like going from 60 mph to 0 mph. A study shows that trying to get yourself to calm down will only make the anxiety worse because then you fight against it. However, you can beat it when you understand how panic works, what it is and the role your brain has in making it worse.

Excitement and anxiety feel the same in your body. When people ask the author about how she manages her nerves during public speaking, she tells them that she has never gotten over her fears and nerves but instead uses them to her advantage. She terms her nervousness as excitement because physiologically anxiety and excitement are the exact same thing. The only difference lies in what your mind calls them. The author still experiences the same nervousness whenever she is about to speak publicly but just channels it in a positive direction. Even as her confidence grows with each speech that is delivered, her physical response remains the same which makes her think that maybe this is her body's way of getting ready to do something cool. Therefore, she started telling herself that she was only getting excited instead of getting nervous.

Say you're excited

The trick explained above is more precisely called 'anxiety reappraisal'. Reframing your anxiety as excitement is a simple yet powerful way of dealing with it. Studies prove the effectiveness of this trick which can be used to perform better under any stressful condition.

Telling yourself that you are excited does not actually lower the feelings surging through your body but it just gives your mind an explanation that empowers you. This prevents the feelings of nervousness from escalating and helps you stay in control. Your brain will just think that you are excited which will ring no alarm bells and your body will start to calm down as you begin to move.

As soon as you start feeling anxious, 5-4-3-2-1 tell yourself that you are just excited and push yourself to move forward. The rest will be under control. Exerting yourself allows your prefrontal cortex to take control and focus you on a positive explanation.

"You are braver than you believe, stronger than you seem, and smarter than you think."

-AA Milne

Beat fear

The author cured herself of the fear of flying using the 5-second rule and a specific form of anxiety reappraisal that is called 'anchor thoughts'. This technique works by thinking of a thought relevant to the trip that will anchor the person once fear sets in. the author starts thinking about the trip and any things she is excited about in relation to the trip before going on one. Once she has a specific image in mind, the rest settles itself automatically.

This technique is called the 'If, then' rule by researchers and is a way to create a backup plan in advance in order to remain in control of the situation. Plan A is not to get nervous but even if you do (which you might) you can use the 5-second rule and your anchor thought to beat your fear. This technique can boost your success rates by three times. By using anchoring thoughts, you are giving your mind the context it is looking for so that it does not escalate the fear. Once you practice this regularly, you will train your mind to default to the positive, and the excitement attached with the optimistic outlook, instead of getting bogged down with fear.

When you enter a conversation managing a fear, you cannot be your best because part of your mind is busy managing that fear in real time. When you have an anchor thought, it helps you eliminate the fear the moment that you notice your mind drifting towards it. You can take back control just as quickly as fear overcomes you.

Master your mind and anything is possible.

Part 5; Courage Changes Everything
How to become the most fulfilled person you know
The ending chapters of this book focus on confidence and how it can be built using daily acts of courage. You will also learn about a surprising connection between confidence and personality and how everyday courage helps you discover your passion. This is because the courage discovered as a result of the 5-second rule will help you pursue what is in your heart. You will also explore what creates deep and meaningful connections in relationships and

why courage is a critical component of this process.

There will always be someone who can't see your worth. Don't let it be you.

Building real confidence

Confidence is not a personality trait rather it is a skill. It simply means that you believe in yourself, your ideas and your capabilities. The people who seem confident from outside are usually the most insecure from the inside while the quietest of the people may be the most confident.

The author narrates the story of one of her followers who used the 5-second rule to approach and strike a conversation with the CEO of his company, who was also a hero for him. This person is then able to secure a job interview by sharing his ideas with the CEO during the conversation which might change the trajectory of his life for the good. However, his exuberance was not necessarily about meeting the CEO but more about how good it feels to when you honor your desires and take control of your life. He was radiating because he knew he could count on himself which was boosting his confidence.

Confidence is created by small things you do every day that build trust in yourself. A good life is made up of small steps which may be little steps in learning to trust yourself but they are the most exhilarating moves that you can make for your confidence. Small things are not small at all. They are the most important and they add up.

Confidence build when you do things that affirm your sense of self, particularly those that you do not normally like to do. If you find yourself making excuses such as 'I am an introvert' and 'this sort of thing does not come naturally to me' then you must remember that there is nothing that comes 'naturally' and that nothing about your life and personality is fixed. Nothing comes naturally until you practice it. You have the ability to improve, change or enrich every single aspect of your life through action. According to a Cambridge University professor, while some of our traits are more fixed and automatic, others can be adjusted in order to advance a core project through deliberate action.

Although it may seem difficult the first time you do anything, you must remember that we are all capable of 'acting out of character' when the time comes and when it serves an important purpose. And the most important purpose the author can think of is improving your life in ways that make you come alive and feel happy and fulfilled. Your acts of courage may not be earth shattering but they will definitely shatter your self-doubt.

If you have the courage to take action then your confidence will follow. The more that you use the rule, the faster your confidence will grow. Stop focusing on big things, 5-4-3-2-1-GO on the smallest things and you will see that these moments are not actually that small. These small actions will create a ripple effect that change your life and the payoff that you get is everything; confidence, control and a sense of pride that feels damn good.

Speak from your heart, even if your voice shakes.

Pursuing passion

As opportunities start to appear, you will find that the 5-second rule is an incredible tool. Finding your passion is an active process. Some people are unable to find their passion because they are unable to get out of their thoughts and move into action. The 5-second rule can be used to push yourself to start exploring and lean into opportunities as they appear.

Your curiosity is how your instincts get you to pay attention to what your heart really cares about. Look out for something that you can't stop thinking about and your emotions of envy because these are the things that you really want for yourself. Next, you should explore that subject of interest. Talk to people, take classes, watch video tutorials and make a plan. You discover your passion like this; 5-4-3-2-1 explore until you bump into it!

Build momentum

As you start exploring and start planning, one thing will lead to another and soon you will experience a momentum building. You might get a little overwhelmed in the beginning but you will thank yourself for finding the courage to trust your heart and explore what fascinates you. Momentum builds from something small which leads to bigger things in life. As your exploration picks up momentum, you will move into the next phase which is actually pursuing your passion full-time.

Turning your passion into a life-changing project requires careful planning and deep thinking. You may even torture yourself for a while before moving forward. You must ask yourself, 'Am I ready to commit to this?' instead of 'Do I feel ready to commit to this?' because you will never FEEL ready. The moment you answer yes to the question 'Am I ready to commit to this?' you should use the 5-second rule to give yourself the final push that you need so badly.

The author believes that you can make anything happen as long as you listen to your heart, do the work and give up on the timeline. There is no expiration date on discovering and expressing the power of you. It starts with a belief in yourself and that belief is grounded in the courage to push yourself. The answers are inside of you if you have the courage to listen. You are remarkable in your own way and it all starts by listening what's inside of you and ends with the courage to go where it leads.

You must follow it.

Don't tell people your dreams. Show them.

Enrich your relationships

Leave nothing important unsaid. Intimacy takes courage. To risk getting emotional or upsetting someone so that you can express how you feel can be scary but the outcome is worth it.

Waiting for the right time to get real in your relationships is a fool's errand because there is no right time to ask the hard questions, express your emotions or take the time to truly listen. It may even be the question of ending the silence between you and some other person in your life but remember that it only takes five seconds to change your life.

To feel worthy, you must first make your own instincts worthy of your attention and effort. Silence is a problem because choosing not to say what you feel creates 'cognitive dissonance' between what you truly believe in and what you actually do in the moment. Those problems build up and can ultimately break your relationships. Silence creates distance and the truth is the shortest distance between two people that creates real connection.

Sometimes, there is no next time. We often fail to appreciate the profound power held inside the smallest moments of our relationships.

All our dreams can come true if we have the courage to pursue them.

- Walt Disney

The power of you

"You've always had the power my dear, you just had to learn it for yourself"

-Glinda, the Wizard of Oz

All of the people who move forward and honor their instincts with action know that they do not feel like it but they still move simply because they know the secret to greatness. Whenever your heart speaks, you must 5-4-3-2-1 and move to honor the voice. These people take action because the consequences of the alternative of doing so are unacceptable. The biggest risk in this situation is to die before you have actually pushed yourself to live.

You can move mountains, indeed. This life of yours is not going to happen again. You cannot change the past but in five seconds, you can change the future. That is the power of every day courage. One moment of courage can change your day. One day can change your life and your life can change the world.

There is greatness in you and the time to reveal it is now!
5-4-3-2-1-GO...

Conclusion

Thank you again for downloading this book!

I hope this book was able to help you to get more insight to all the key components of the book in less time.

The next step is to try out the practical approaches listed in this book and find the ones that work best for you.

Just wanted to say thank you once again for purchasing and reading my book.

I truly do appreciate it!

Best Wishes,

EpicRead

Printed in Great Britain
by Amazon